Natural Disasters

Landslides

by

Anne Ylvisaker

Consultant:
Lynn Highland
United States Geological Survey

CAPSTONE BOOKS
an imprint of Capstone Press
Mankato, Minnesota

Capstone Books are published by Capstone Press
151 Good Counsel Drive, P.O. Box 669, Mankato, Minnesota 56002
www.capstonepress.com

Library of Congress Cataloging-in-Publication Data
Ylvisaker, Anne.
    Landslides/by Anne Ylvisaker.
    p. cm.—(Natural disasters)
    Includes bibliographical references and index.
    Contents: Landslides—Why landslides happen—The power of
a landslide—Famous landslides—Surviving a landslide.
    ISBN 0-7368-1507-4 (hardcover)
    ISBN 0-7368-4906-8 (paperback)
    1. Landslides—Juvenile literature. [1. Landslides.] I. Title.
II. Series: Natural disasters (Capstone Press)
QE599.A2 Y59 2003
363.34—dc21   2002010887

Summary: Describes how and why landslides happen, the damage they cause,
ways to avoid and survive them, and famous landslides of the past.

Editorial Credits
Matt Doeden, editor; Karen Risch, product planning editor; Timothy Halldin,
    series designer; Patrick Dentinger, book designer; Jo Miller, photo researcher

Photo Credits
AP/Wide World Photos/Roger J. Wyan, 22
Bruce Coleman, Inc./Jeff Foott, 10; Keith Gunnar, 13; Janis Burger, 38–39
Corbis, 30; Sygma/Australian News LTD, 4 (both), 7; James A. Sugar, 9;
    Jonathan Blair, 15; AFP, 16, 29; Paul A. Souders, 18; Gary Braasch, 24, 26–27;
    Bettmann, 32; Reuters NewMedia, Inc., 34; Kevin R. Morris, 36
Photo Network/Mary Messenger, 21
Unicorn Stock Photos/A. Ramey, cover
The Viesti Collection, Inc./Peter Bennett, 40
Visuals Unlimited/Sylvester Allred, 44; NGDC, 47

2 3 4 5 6 08 07 06 05

Table of Contents

Chapter 1

Landslides

In 1997, Stuart and Sally Driver lived next to a ski lodge in the mountains near Thredbo, Australia. On the night of August 1, an underground water spring burst from a mountain above their home. Cold spring water gushed out of the mountain. It loosened rocks and dirt, which fell down the slope. A landslide had begun.

The landslide grew as it sped down the mountain. Rocks crashed into the ski lodge near the Drivers' home. Pieces of the ski lodge slammed into their roof. Stuart and Sally woke suddenly. They tried to hold on to one another, but the rush of water that followed

In 1997, an avalanche near Thredbo, Australia, destroyed a ski lodge and several homes.

the landslide swept Sally away. Stuart was trapped in a small area that was partly filled with cold spring water. He had to hold his head out of the water to breathe.

Rescue workers arrived quickly. They saw a disaster area filled with rocks, mud, concrete slabs, and twisted wreckage. They immediately began the search for survivors. But they believed everyone was dead.

Two days after the landslide, rescue workers heard an unusual sound. They followed the noise to a small hole in the wreckage. The sound was Stuart, shouting for help. The rescue workers immediately began digging to free Stuart. But they had to be very careful. They did not want the wreckage to crash down on top of him. Twelve hours later, they pulled him to safety. Stuart had been trapped for about 65 hours.

Rescue workers continued to search for other survivors, including Sally. They did not find anyone. Eighteen people died in the disaster. Stuart was the only survivor.

Rescuers pulled Stuart Driver from the wreckage of the Thredbo landslide. He was the only survivor.

About Landslides

Landslides happen when dirt, rock, or mud suddenly falls or slides down a slope. Mudslides are the most common type of landslides. Heavy rain turns soil into mud, which may begin flowing down a slope. The mud loosens more soil and rock as it travels.

7

All of the material carried down a slope during a landslide is called debris. Mud and rocks are the main types of debris. Other landslide debris can include trees that have been torn out of the ground, crushed buildings, and even cars. On steep slopes, debris can travel at speeds of more than 130 miles (210 kilometers) per hour. At these speeds, landslides can crush buildings and bury entire towns in seconds.

Landslides can also happen under water. These submarine landslides occur in coastal areas where land slopes from the edge of the water. An earthquake in 1964 caused a submarine landslide in the harbor of Valdez, Alaska. Many buildings and shipping docks were pulled into the water by the force of the slide.

All of the material carried down a slope during a landslide is called debris.

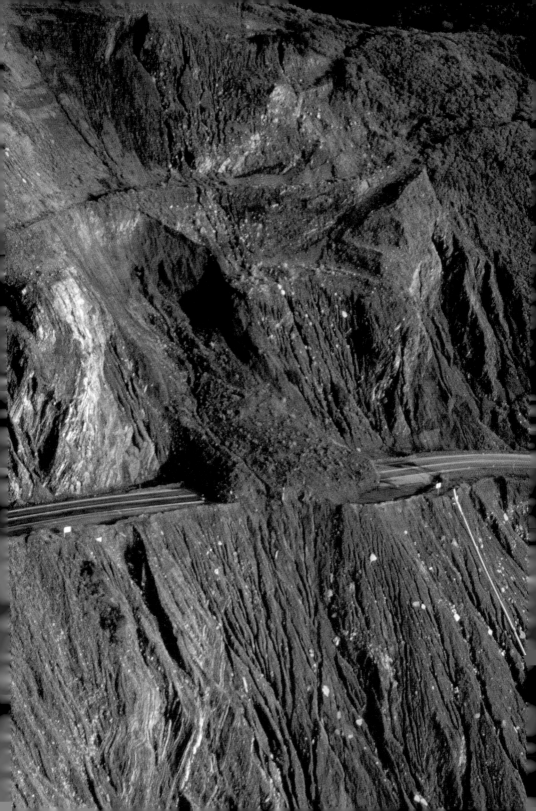

Chapter 2

Why Landslides Happen

Thousands of landslides happen around the world every year. Many landslides occur in mountain areas where no people live. These landslides often go unnoticed. But a landslide that hits a town or city can cause deaths and millions of dollars in damage.

The ground is made of several layers. The surface layer is soil and rock. Trees and plants grow in this layer. Layers below the surface are made of clay, limestone, sandstone, or other types of rock and soil. The bottom layer is usually solid rock. In some coastal areas, the bottom layer is made up of soil and other loose material called fill.

Landslides often start when loose soil begins sliding down a slope.

Layers of the ground usually hold together well, but sometimes, the surface layer becomes unstable. If an unstable surface layer rests on a slope, gravity may pull it down and begin a landslide.

Water

Soil needs some water to hold together. Soil that is too dry can blow away in the wind. Soil that is is too wet can lose its hold on the layer below it.

Many landslides happen during heavy rain. Water soaks the surface layer. The soil turns to mud. Mud is heavier and more slippery than dry soil. On a steep slope, mud may flow downward to begin a mudslide.

Water can also start a landslide in rocky areas. On a slope, rocks stay in one place because of friction. This force between two objects prevents gravity from pulling the rocks down the slope. Water can reduce the force of friction and cause rocks to slide. These rocks can knock other rocks loose and begin a landslide. Yearly cycles of water freezing and

Water mixes with soil to create mud. Mud may flow down a slope and start a mudslide.

melting can loosen rocks and cause them to fall.

Water can also soak into a layer of soil below the surface. The water can turn a lower layer into mud and reduce friction. This effect can cause the surface layer to come loose and begin a landslide.

Erosion

Erosion happens when wind, water, or other forces wear away the surface layer of the ground. Wind is a major cause of erosion. Strong winds often blow across mountains, carrying away dry soil. This erosion can weaken the grip between layers of soil.

Running water is another source of erosion. Rainwater carries soil as it pours down a slope. Water from melting snow runs down many mountains during spring and summer. Over time, this erosion can cause layers of ground to loosen and slide.

Fires can cause landslides. Fires burn away the trees and plants on a mountainside. Fire

Erosion can cause rocks to come loose from the ground and fall.

also can change the way layers of soil hold together. These changes can increase the chances of a landslide.

Trees and plants help prevent erosion. Their roots hold soil in place. Many mountain slopes have few plants and trees. The soil on these slopes may erode quickly. These slopes are often at the highest risk of landslides.

Earthquakes and Volcanoes

Earthquakes and volcanoes often cause the largest landslides. An earthquake happens when plates deep below the Earth's surface rub against one another. The ground above the plates shakes violently. Layers of soil and rock can break apart. When an earthquake takes place near a slope, gravity pulls down the debris.

A volcano spits out lava, steam, and hot gases when it erupts. The heat from an eruption can melt snow and ice on the top of a mountain. The water turns the soil into mud. The mud mixes with lava, ash, and dust from the explosion. This mixture, called lahar or volcanic mudflow, rushes down the slope. The hot lahar can burn and bury anything in its path.

Lava that hardens after a volcanic eruption often breaks apart easily. A landslide of this hardened lava is called a volcano edifice collapse.

Earthquakes can loosen large amounts of rock and soil.

Chapter 3

The Power of a Landslide

Landslides in the United States cause more than $1 billion in property damage each year. They often cause deaths as well. Organized rescue teams in the United States help to reduce the number of people killed in landslides. This number is often much higher in countries that are not as well prepared for disasters.

Mudslides

Mudslides are among the most destructive types of landslides. Mudslides usually occur in dry mountain areas. Soil in dry areas often

---

Landslides cause more than $1 billion in property damage each year.

cannot hold much water. Heavy rains quickly turn dry soil to mud. The mud is heavy and slippery. Gravity pulls it down the slope. Soon, large rivers of mud form. Mudslides that include large amounts of rocks, trees, and other materials are called debris flows.

Mudslides can wash away people, animals, buildings, cars, and crops. The mud gathers soil and debris as it moves down the slope. It becomes thicker. This thick mud can bury everything in its path. People caught in a mudslide may be buried. Many people buried in a mudslide are never found.

The most dangerous mudslides happen after volcanic eruptions. These mudslides often cover huge areas. The mud may be so hot that it can burn the clothing and skin off people caught in its path.

Falling Rock
Large rocks sometimes break loose and fall from a cliff or slope. These small landslides

Large rivers of mud can block roads.

Rockslides can cover and destroy roads.

are sometimes called rockfalls or rockslides. They usually affect only a small area. But a rockslide that hits a building or a car can be deadly.

Rockslides can begin in several ways. Water or wind can erode the ground holding a large rock. Rain also can cause rocks to come loose.

Noise vibrations are another major cause of rockslides. Loud noises such as thunder or even passing traffic can cause a rock to fall.

In the United States, rockslides are most common in California and Colorado. Many homes in these states are built on steep slopes. Many roads are built along the bottom edge of tall cliffs. Rocks falling from these slopes and cliffs can crush homes and cars. They can also block major roads. Sometimes large sections of rock and land break away from a hillside or cliff. Entire neighborhoods of homes can be pushed into valleys.

The weight and speed of sliding rock can also cause floods. In 1963, a landslide in Italy sent tons of debris into a lake. The debris caused a wave about 330 feet (100 meters) high. The wave flooded the area, killing 3,000 people.

Chapter 4

Famous Landslides

People often have little or no warning that a landslide is about to happen. Scientists try to predict when and where landslides are likely, but these warnings often are for very large areas. No one knows exactly when or where a landslide will begin.

Mount Saint Helens, 1980

The largest landslide in recorded history followed the eruption of a volcano in the state of Washington. Mount Saint Helens erupted on May 18, 1980. Lava, steam, and hot gases melted the snow on top of the mountain. Water, lava, and ash mixed to form lahar.

The eruption of Mount Saint Helens started the largest landslide in recorded history.

This mud rushed down the mountain. It destroyed large areas of forest and swept away many buildings and houses.

The Mount Saint Helens mudslide ran for more than 23 miles (37 kilometers). It went through nearby Spirit Lake. The impact sent millions of gallons of water down the mountain. The water mixed with the lahar,

The landslide after the Mount Saint Helens eruption destroyed hundreds of thousands of trees.

increasing the size and power of the mudslide. The mudslide continued through the Toutle River Valley. It blocked rivers, burned forests, covered roads, and destroyed homes. More than 50 people died in the disaster. Countless trees and animals were killed.

Alpine Landslides, 2000

In October 2000, heavy rains fell in the Alps in Italy, Switzerland, and France. Some areas of these mountains received as much as 24 inches (61 centimeters) of rain in two days. The rain caused flooding and several landslides.

A large rock broke off from a mountain during the heavy rains. The rock sped down the slope and destroyed a dam near the village of Gondo, Switzerland. A wall of water and debris then slammed into the village, destroying almost half of its buildings and damaging many more. Officials believe 13 people died in the disaster.

Landslides and floods also damaged other villages in the area. Four houses in Stalden were swept away. Dozens of people died. Thousands more were forced to leave their homes.

Peru Mudslide, 1970

Mount Huascaran once towered above the town of Yungay, Peru. In 1970, an earthquake shook

In 2000, landslides in Italy killed dozens of people.

28

the mountain. A huge block of ice broke loose from the top of the mountain and began an avalanche. Scientists guess that the block was more than 3,000 feet (900 meters) wide and 5,000 feet (1,500 meters) long.

The ice crashed down the mountain, picking up rock, dirt, and other debris. Much of the ice melted as it slid down the slope. The water mixed with dirt to create a huge mudslide that rushed down the mountain at speeds of more than 130 miles (210 kilometers) per hour. The mudslide buried the town of Yungay, killing almost 20,000 people there.

The mudslide also hit several other towns. Together, the earthquake and mudslide killed nearly 70,000 people.

Aberfan Landslide, 1966
Aberfan was a coal-mining town in the country of Wales. Miners worked in coal mines beneath the town. The miners piled tons of waste material called slag on a hill. Over time, this slag heap grew larger.

In 1970, a landslide on Peru's Mount Huascaran killed nearly 70,000 people.

By 1966, the pile stood more than 600 feet (183 meters) tall.

On October 21, 1966, children were attending Aberfan's school. The school building stood near the bottom of the slag heap. Heavy rains had fallen in Aberfan for two days. The slag mixed with water and became muddy. That morning, the slag heap became unstable. A mudslide began, sending 500,000 tons (453,600 metric tons) of waste down into Aberfan.

The school was the first building in the mudslide's path. The debris buried the school. All 116 children inside were killed. The disaster also destroyed 20 homes. A total of 144 people died in the mudslide.

Waste from a coal mine covered the town of Aberfan, Wales, after a 1966 landslide.

Chapter 5

Surviving a Landslide

People cannot prevent landslides from happening. Scientists cannot even predict exactly when or where a landslide will happen. But people can follow some safety practices to protect themselves from landslides.

Warnings and Prevention

Governments around the world try to warn people about areas that are at high risk of landslides. Falling rocks are a common problem in California. Workers climb cliffs along the state's highways to look for loose

Landslides are dangerous because they are so difficult to predict.

rocks that could start rockslides. They carefully release these rocks down the cliff. Workers build heavy steel nets along some roads. The nets catch or slow down falling rocks before they can crash onto the road.

Japan has many active volcanoes. Even small eruptions from these volcanoes can cause large mudslides. Many towns near Japan's volcanoes surround themselves with large steel and concrete walls designed to stop mudslides.

Japanese scientists closely watch the volcanoes. They look for signs that an eruption is likely. If the danger is high, the government may ask people nearby to evacuate the area. These people must leave their homes and move to a safer place until the danger passes.

Survival

People can take steps to protect themselves from landslides. Hikers and climbers should

---

Hikers should avoid areas that appear to have unstable rocks.

always pay attention to landslide warnings.
People driving along cliffs and steep hills
should look for warning signs. Drivers should
watch especially closely in areas where
rockslides are common.

People caught in landslides may not have
time to protect themselves. People who see

Roads along steep hills are at high risk of landslides.

debris coming down a slope should try to move to an area of high ground. They should stand behind a large, stable object such as a large tree or a boulder. These safety practices can be helpful during small landslides. But

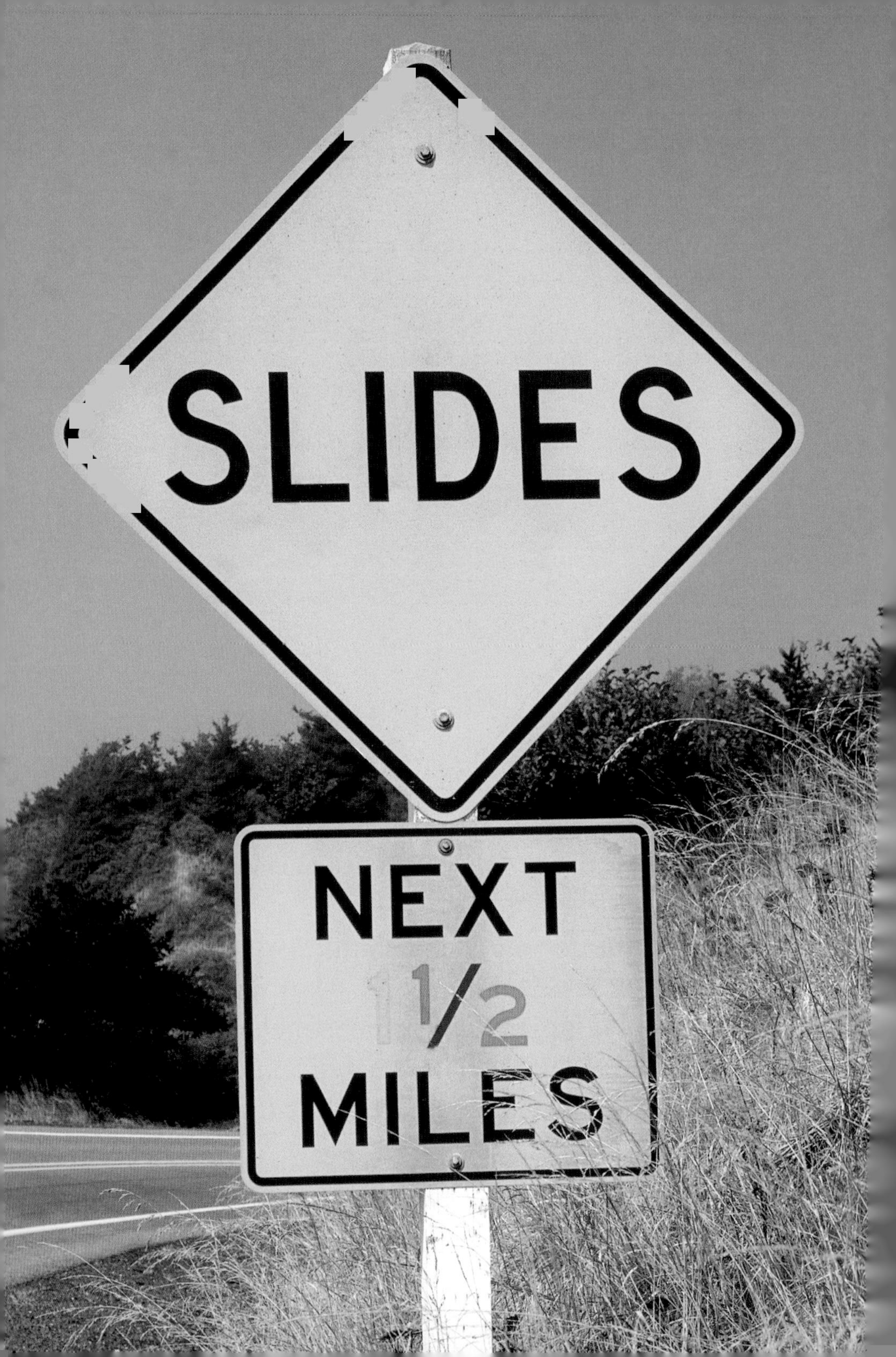
SLIDES
NEXT
1/2
MILES

during a large landslide, no amount of safety measures may be helpful.

People who see a mudslide coming may be able to outrun the mud. On steep slopes, mudslides travel very fast. But they lose speed as the slope becomes less steep. People who are caught in a mudslide should move their arms in a swimming motion. They should try to keep their head above the mud at all times. These safety measures cannot completely protect people from mudslides. But they can help reduce the number of lives lost to these natural disasters.

People should pay close attention to landslide warning signs.

Words to Know

debris (duh-BREE)—rocks, dirt, and other objects that fall down a slope during a landslide

erosion (ee-ROH-zhuhn)—the wearing away of land by water or wind

evacuate (ee-VAK-yoo-ate)—to leave an area during a time of danger

friction (FRIK-shuhn)—a force that holds two objects together; friction helps keep layers of soil together on a slope.

gravity (GRAV-uh-tee)—the force that pulls objects toward Earth

lahar (luh-HAR)—material that flows down a volcano's slope after water mixes with volcanic debris

slag (SLAG)—waste material pulled from a coal mine

To Learn More

Engelbert, Phillis. *Dangerous Planet: The Science of Natural Disasters.* Detroit: UXL, 2001.

Goodwin, Peter. *Landslides, Slumps, and Creep.* A First Book. New York: Franklin Watts, 1997.

Newson, Joyce E. *Natural Disasters.* Nature's Record-Breakers. Milwaukee: Gareth Stevens, 2002.

Redmond, Jim, and Ronda Redmond. *Landslides and Avalanches.* Nature on the Rampage. Austin, Texas: Steadwell Books, 2002.

Useful Addresses ←

**Federal Emergency Management
Agency (FEMA)**
500 C Street SW
Washington, DC 20472-0001

National Landslide Information Center
USGS
Mail Stop 966, Box 25046
Denver Federal Center
Denver, CO 80225

United States Geological Survey (USGS)
509 National Center
Reston, VA 20192

Internet Sites

Do you want to learn more about landslides?
Visit the FACT HOUND at *http://www.facthound.com*

FACT HOUND can track down many sites to help you.
All the FACT HOUND sites are hand-selected by Capstone
Press editors. FACT HOUND will fetch the best, most accurate
information to answer your questions.

IT IS EASY! IT IS FUN!
1) Go to *http://www.facthound.com*
2) Type in: 0736815074
3) Click on "FETCH IT" and FACT HOUND will put you on
the trail of several helpful links.

**You can also search by subject or book title. So, relax
and let our pal FACT HOUND do the research for you!**

Index